Wild Plants in the City

WILD PLANTS IN THE CITY

Nancy M. Page
Richard E. Weaver, Jr.

Drawings: Robert Opdyke
Photographs: Nancy M. Page

Quadrangle/The New York Times Book Co.

Library of Congress Catalog Card Number: 74-29034

International Standard Book Number: 0-8129-0557-1

Contents

Foreword

To anyone who has done any traveling, it should certainly be obvious that the associations of plants, or "vegetation," which cover the land are quite diverse, both in terms of structure and species composition. This diversity is due to a complex interaction of many environmental factors including climate, soils, and light. The various species of plants are adapted to survive and flourish under the combination of factors peculiar to each of the multitude of habitats on the earth. Occasionally, a single factor may be more important than all of the others in determining the character of the vegetation at a given site. For example, desert vegetation is composed of plants which are able to survive with a minimum of water, and which possess structures, such as fleshy leaves or stems, which enable them to conserve the existing supply. In general, desert plants are also widely spaced, largely as a result of competition for water. The situation in other vegetation types may be considerably more complex. In a forest for example, the trees strongly modify the amount and type of light, moisture, and nutrients available to the understory plants.

When land and its covering of vegetation is disturbed in some way or another, such as through farming, fire, or construction, the balance of environmental factors is altered. Thus, if the vegetation is allowed to recover, the first stages of revegetation will include kinds of plants that were not among the original components. With each succeeding stage, each one made up of a different group of plants, the original balance of environmental factors is gradually restored, and eventually the structure and species composition of the vegetation will be more or less the same as before the disturbance.

This gradual process by which land is revegetated after disturbance is known as "succession." The stages of succession have been well worked out in many parts of the world. The kinds of plants constituting each stage are remarkably uniform for a given vegetation type in a given geographical area. In general, the pioneers in succession are annual, or short-lived perennial, herbaceous plants which grow rapidly, have easily dispersed seeds, and are intolerant of shading and competition from other plants. At least in forested parts of the eastern United States, these are gradually replaced by slower growing, more shade tolerant plants, including some woody species; finally, shade tolerant, woody species predominate. Most of the vegetation types in a city such as Boston are ones in various stages of succession. Some are unique to urban conditions; others are similar to those of disturbed sites elsewhere.

By far the bulk of the spontaneous vegetation of this or any other city is contained in vacant lots, most of which at one time or another were occupied by buildings. The soil of recently cleared lots is generally very poor, consisting primarily of "fill" and rubble, with little organic matter present. Still, plants begin to appear almost immediately after a building has been torn down. A large number of species may invade, but in Boston at least, Mugwort (*Artemisia vulgaris*) is usually predominant. Other common plants in new lots include Clovers (*Trifolium* spp.), Sweetclovers (*Melilotus* spp.), Horseweed (*Conyza canadensis*), Ragweed (*Ambrosia artemisiifolia*), and various grasses. Seedlings of tree species, particularly those of the Tree of Heaven (*Ailanthus altissima*), are usually also present from the beginning. As the herbaceous plants grow, die down, and decompose, they add organic matter to the soil, improving it and theoretically making it possible for other plant species to become established. In a few years the herbaceous vegetation becomes quite dense, consisting primarily of the same plant species as were present in the pioneering stage; tree saplings are often present. However, succession is rarely allowed to proceed much further, due to disturbance of the sites through new building construction. Thus we can only speculate on the nature of later successional stages and the ultimate vegetation of vacant lots. At least one area was seen in Boston which was almost forest-like in appearance, with trees to two feet in diameter. Native species, such as Red Oak (*Quercus rubra*), Black Oak (*Q. velutina*), and Black Cherry (*Prunus serotina*) predominated, but weedy, introduced species including Tree of Heaven, Norway Maple (*Acer platanoides*), and Horsechestnut (*Aesculus hippocastanum*) were also present. This "forest" may represent a close approximation to the ultimate vegetation to be expected on a grown-up lot.

Along expressway embankments and other areas, including

vacant lots, which are subject to frequent mowing, various grasses are often the major component of the vegetation. Plants which are able to reproduce vegetatively, that is in general by means other than seeds (e.g., stolons, runners, rhizomes, offsets), are at an advantage in such situations. They are able to spread whether or not their tops, including flowers and seeds, are cut off. Many grasses, including some of the common lawn species, spread rapidly by vegetative means. Once they become established, grasses cover the ground so closely that seedlings of other plants are unable to grow. Therefore, periodically mown grassy fields are generally devoid of trees at any stage; only a few species of broad-leaved herbs are commonly present, including Butter and Eggs (*Linaria vulgaris*), Evening Primrose (*Oenothera biennis*), Tansy (*Tanacetum vulgare*), Goldenrod (*Solidago* spp.), Mullein (*Verbascum thapsus*), Milkweed (*Asclepias syriaca*), Black-eyed Susan (*Rudbeckia hirta*), and Field Daisy (*Chrysanthemum leucanthemum*). Even if they are not torn up, these areas will not often proceed further as far as a succession of vegetation is concerned.

Sidewalk cracks offer one of the most severe environments for plant growth in the city. The soil is poor if any is present at all, moisture is scarce, and temperature varies from very hot in the summer to cold in the winter. Despite these inhospitable conditions, not to mention the trampling by countless unsympathetic feet, a surprisingly large number of plant species survive and even flourish here. Various grasses, Clovers (*Trifolium* spp.), Plantains (*Plantago* spp.), as well as Dandelion (*Taraxacum officinale*) and Prostrate Knotweed (*Polygonum aviculare*) are perhaps the most common components of sidewalk crack vegetation. Seedlings of tree species, particularly Tree of Heaven and Norway Maple, often make an appearance, but they seldom succeed because they are unable to tolerate the constant trampling. In more protected cracks, such as those between sidewalks and buildings, these trees have a better chance of surviving the seedling stage. Once established, they generally flourish. In fact, fairly large cracks often support large individuals of a number of woody species. In addition to the two above, Sycamore Maple (*Acer pseudoplatanus*), Siberian Elm (*Ulmus pumila*), American Elm (*U. americana*), Oaks (*Quercus* spp.), and Ashes (*Fraxinus* spp.) are often present.

A small part of Boston's vegetation is more or less "natural," that is, it is made up of the same types of plants as are found in similar, undisturbed sites in the surrounding countryside. The largest and most conspicuous part of this vegetation is found along the water-courses of the city's park system, where extensive areas are dominated by pure stands of the tall grass (to 12 feet tall) locally known as "Reed" or "Bulrush" (*Phragmites communis*). But these are perhaps also the best areas in the city to find what are traditionally known as "wildflowers." During most of the summer there is a progression of bloom from a variety of plants along the water's edge. Arrowheads (*Sagittaria latifolia*) and Pickerelweed (*Pontederia cordata*) grow right in the shallow water. Others such as Purple Loosestrife (*Lythrum salicaria*), Yellow Iris (*Iris pseudacorus*), and Jewelweed (*Impatiens capensis*) are conspicuous along the banks. Cattails (*Typha latifolia*) and various sedges, plants with attractive but not necessarily showy flowers, are also common.

Although "wildflowers" are found in certain specialized habitats, the plants which make up the bulk of the vegetation in inner-city areas are ones which would be popularly termed "weeds." Many people have tried to answer the question: "What is a weed?" We will not. Rather, in this foreword we have pointed out the characteristics which many of these plants have in common and which make them able to colonize cleared sites quickly. Many of them have been associated with man and his actions throughout recorded history. But what was the role of these plants before man appeared? Or, in other words, where did they come from? A standard theory is that they occupied rock outcrops or other natural clearings in the forest, and that they spread when fires or storms opened up the vegetation. A currently more popular theory is that they were not "weedy" in the first place but rather their aggressive tendencies evolved in conjunction with man's developing agriculture. Both theories may be correct in part, but, whatever the case, the plants are with us to stay.

R. E. W., Jr.

Wild Plants in the City

The curious gardens of wild greenery that penetrate cracks in city pavement and grow lushly on old building lots are produced primarily by plants which have immigrated from overseas. A few of them were brought originally to North America as garden plants and have since run wild; but most have slipped in accidentally, their tiny seeds caught in the belongings and supplies of settlers or mixed with the seeds of commercial crops.

Many of the most common weeds we find growing in our cities date far enough back into man's history to have grown in the settlements of ancient Greece and to have marched across Europe with the Romans. Man seems to have produced the conditions they require to flourish, and it is largely through his agency that they have come to assume such prominence throughout the world. By destroying the native vegetation with his towns and roads, fields, pastures and gardens, civilized man has opened the way for weeds; and through his wide-ranging travels, he has helped scatter them to every corner of the earth.

The aggressive characteristics which suit these weedy plants so well to their role as pioneers on cleared sites are the same traits which make them troublesome to gardeners. They are a vigorous, adaptable and tenacious group, well-equipped to seize a quick foothold and thrive where other plants cannot effectively compete with them. They grow well even where soil is deficient in nutrients; often where it is too dry or too moist, too alkaline or too acid. They grow fast enough to surpass their struggling rivals, and they produce unusually abundant seed crops that are apt to fill the surrounding soil with their offspring. Their seeds may be able to lie dormant in the soil for decades, if necessary, until conditions are favorable for germination — and it is suspected that some may last for centuries.

The ease with which the more common weeds have spread from one site to another, and from one part of the world to

1

another, is explained largely by their enormous production of easily dispersed seeds. Nowhere is this more apparent than in the midst of the city, where the bare soil of new sites becomes settled with plants almost overnight. Where do these seeds come from? Some, of course, already may be present in the soil of a new lot, and merely need to be brought closer to the surface through cultivation or bulldozing in order to germinate. Other seeds are carried into a new site with the fill used to cover the foundation of a demolished building, or in the topsoil of a landscape planting. Still others, such as the seeds of Poplar, Dandelion and Milkweed, are equipped with silky parachutes which allow them to float on wind currents from surprisingly long distances. Heavier seeds are dropped by nearby trees, and seeds contained within edible fruits and berries often are scattered by feeding birds and animals. Seeds also are transported on fur and clothing, in mud on the soles of shoes, and on the wheels of vehicles.

This continual invasion of seeds helps explain the speed with which weeds can colonize a bare site, even when there are few other plants in view. Within a year a vacant lot's cleared surface may be covered with plants, and within two years tree saplings may be evident. Within three or four years, an undisturbed lot will be wildly overgrown.

But few lots have an opportunity to actually reforest themselves, for the wild gardens that occupy these areas in the city tend to have a fleeting life. Few are left completely undisturbed for more than two or three years, and they often are replaced so rapidly with one of man's constructions — an asphalted parking lot, a used car lot — that the transformation can be somewhat startling to observers.

The role of these wild plants in the city is an especially ambiguous one. Their presence is often a mark of neglect and poor land management, yet the spontaneous cover they provide is a welcome improvement over the rubble-strewn and dusty wastelands which otherwise would be in view. They raise questions about the use and management of vacant land in the city, for when land is so precious, one wonders how these "wastelands" can be economically and socially expedient.

This is a rather typical building lot, slightly on the seamy side, but already lushly carpeted with Clover and Mugwort (and a less typical Grass) after a few years of growth. The trees springing up along the foundations of adjacent buildings are saplings of the Tree of Heaven.

3

Despite its untidyness, the wild plant growth on these lots has many delightful qualities. Even the seamiest site conveys an intriguing sense of life and a connection with nature that is often lacking in the simplistic environments of contemporary parks and playgrounds. It offers the diversity of an entire community of plants and insects; a surface that has contours, slopes and hollows; and the pleasant surprise of new perspectives and contrasts: the wild lushness of a weedy planter set against the elegance of Copley Square, sheer cliffs rising against the Boston skyline, or an unexpected puddle of water surrounded by Cat-tails and Sedges.

A Note on Trees and Shrubs

In contrast to the vast number of foreign flowers and grasses which were introduced accidentally into the United States and now grow wild in New England towns, the trees and shrubs one is apt to encounter growing wild here are either native plants or plants which were intentionally brought here for cultivation.

On the following pages we have provided only a small sampling of these woody plants; there are many others which most certainly will be encountered as well — such as the Apple, Catalpa, Horsechestnut, Mulberry, and Linden. Exactly what one finds in a particular area depends, of course, on what has been planted there. For instance, the large number of volunteer Maples, Oaks, and Elms which spring up in Boston may be attributed to the use of such trees for street plantings. The potentially large number of other trees and shrubs which may appear, depending on the breadth of local plantings, is suggested by the wide variety of exotic seedlings one finds growing on the Arnold Arboretum grounds and within a few miles of its boundaries.

One group of plants is notably absent in the city, however, and this is the evergreens. Nowhere in urban Boston have we seen seedlings of such evergreens as the Pines or Junipers, which are such prominent pioneers of the old fields in more rural areas.

This is one of a series of tiny ponds we found hidden among piles of fill which had been dumped systematically across a lot along South Huntington Avenue. One day we came upon two wild ducks floating in the center of this pond; on another occasion we flushed a pheasant out of the surrounding vegetation. Wildlife may be more plentiful on this lot than most others because of its proximity to the Muddy River.

On the pond's edges grow Willows, Cat-tails, Sedges, and — in mid-summer — a bright array of wildflowers, such as Loosestrife, Tansy, and Queen Anne's Lace.

4

From the road this waterfront area looks like an abandoned parking lot; but as one approaches the back of the site, small ponds (such as this one rimmed by Cat-tails and beautiful Grasses) appear in shallow depressions.

A miniature meadow, created by a weedy planter in Copley Square, stands in strange juxtaposition to the urban surroundings. The planter was dominated by Clover, Yellow Wood Sorrel, and Horseweed, but we collected 30 different kinds of plants from this site. Shortly after this photograph was taken, the weeds were removed and a cover of sod laid down, producing a neater, but less interesting, landscape.

These spectacular cliffs are one of the finest natural features of Boston now in private hands, and they should be carefully preserved. They form an outcrop along one side of Mission Hill, known as "The Ledge." Looking across the old quarry which lies on one side of The Ledge, one sees the startling juxtaposition of natural and man-made landscapes pictured at right.

In the quarry grow trees of many kinds, such as the Tree of Heaven, Norway and Sycamore Maples, Black Locust, Oaks, Poplars, and Ashes. Pin Oaks and Gray Birches (and even occasional ferns) grow out of the crevices in the cliffs. On the rim above the cliffs are a few Black Cherries, a Red Maple or two, and a large, rather flat field covered with flowers of many different kinds.

How to Use This Handbook

This handbook should be useful in identifying plants in cities throughout the northeastern United States, even though our observations were made almost entirely in Boston. We have not attempted to include all of the wild plants that we encountered. Rather, we have selected those which are most common and/or conspicuous, as well as some which are of unusual interest for one reason or another. Each plant included is represented by one or more illustrations. Identifying features such as height and leaf dimensions, and pertinent facts such as habitat and area of origin are included in the text accompanying the illustrations.

The plants are divided into four categories:

Herbaceous Flowering Plants	Trees and Shrubs
Grasses and Grasslike Plants	Ferns

The plants in the first category, being by far the most numerous, are again subdivided according to the color of their flowers, the categories being:

white	magenta	orange
pink	blue	greenish
purple	yellow	inconspicuous

To find a particular plant, simply flip through the pertinent category, using the illustrations as a means of identification.

To further aid in the identification of the herbaceous flowering plants, the following "key" may be used. This key consists of a series of diagrams showing generalized leaf shapes, and these are divided into eight main groups. The individual groups consist of one to five leaf types, representing variation within each of these groups. When identifying an unknown plant, first try to decide into which of the eight groups its leaves *best* fit. Remember that the diagrams are not meant to look *exactly* like actual leaves, but only to give general impressions of the leaf shapes.

The plants within each leaf-shape group are further subdivided according to flower color. Especially with the larger groups, this key will not lead to a specific identification; but it will help to narrow down the choices. It still will be necessary to look through at least a portion of the guide.

Along Washington Street one sees this example of pioneering vegetation squeezing through the cracks and crevices of an entirely paved site. The largest trees are Lombardy Poplars which were 15 or 20 feet tall when this photograph was taken in 1973. There also was a mature Quaking Aspen, as well as smaller saplings of the Tree of Heaven, Norway Maple, and Lombardy Poplar.

11

Greenish or inconspicuous flowers
Pineapple-weed, page 204
Ragweed, page 206
Mugwort, page 207

White or pink flowers
Galinsoga, page 159
Chickweed, page 160
White Campion, page 161
Bladder Campion, page 162
Asters, page 164
Fleabane, page 165
Smartweeds, page 169
Japanese Knotweed, page 166
Bouncing Bet, page 170
Milkweed, page 172

Yellow or orange flowers
St. John's-wort, page 190
Mullein, page 193
Evening Primrose, page 194
Goldenrods, page 195
Hawkweed, page 198
Black-eyed-susan, page 200
Touch-me-not, page 203

Blue, purple, or magenta flowers
Asters, page 164
Nightshade, page 174
Burdock, page 176
Loosestrife, page 179
Vipers Bugloss, page 180
Dayflower, page 182

White, pink, purple, or yellow flowers
Clovers, pages 156, 157, 173

White or yellow flowers
Sweet Clovers, page 156

Yellow flowers
Wood Sorrel, page 188

Yellow flowers
Buttercups, page 184

Greenish or inconspicuous flowers
Beggar-ticks, page 205

White flowers
Ox-eye Daisy, page 163

Yellow flowers
Celandine, page 186
Winter Cress, page 191
Sow-thistle, page 196

13

Herbaceous
Flowering Plants

Field Bindweed — *Convolvulus arvensis*

Naturalized from Europe

HEIGHT: trailing or twining stems, 1-3 feet long.

LEAVES: 1-2 inches long.

FLOWERS: white or pale pink, 1-2 inches across. June to July.

Trailing along the ground of building lots and old fields, the Field Bindweed with its lovely trumpet-shaped flowers can be a most charming sight. But Field Bindweed tends to be more renowned for its aggression than for its flowers, because this is a particularly troublesome vine in cultivated fields and gardens throughout the United States.

It may take 20 to 30 cultivations to eradicate Bindweed from a field. Its roots are capable of penetrating soil up to 20 feet deep, and new plants are formed along a creeping, perennial root system that may spread over an area as large as 30 square yards in a single season. Bindweed also reproduces freely from seeds. It is particularly persistent in rich, heavy soil on the alkaline side.

Morning-glory Family (Convolvulaceae)

16

Queen Anne's Lace — *Daucus carota*

Naturalized from Europe

HEIGHT: up to 3 feet.

LEAVES: feathery, finely cut.

FLOWERS: white, in conspicuous flat clusters 3-4 inches across. July to September.

This wild relative of the domesticated carrot thrives in almost any sunny, well-drained soil, and it often provides a startling contrast to its bleak surroundings, for it is one of the most elegant plants to appear in Boston fields and building lots. Apparently Queen Anne's Lace came to the United States with early settlers, since it was already present in New England by the seventeenth century. Today its delicate foliage and large, umbrella-shaped, white flower clusters are a familiar sight in old dry fields and waste places throughout North America.

In the first year of growth this biennial produces a stout taproot and a low rosette of parsley-like foliage, followed the second year by a flowering stalk which may reach 3 feet tall. After flowering and producing its lightweight seeds, which are easily dispersed by wind, the plant dies.

Parsley Family (Umbelliferae)

17

Yarrow — *Achillea millefolium*

Native to the United States and most parts of the world

HEIGHT: up to 1-2 feet.

LEAVES: 1-10 inches long, deep green, lacy-textured, strongly-scented.

FLOWERS: whitish heads, in flat clusters 2-3 inches across. June to September.

All summer long, Yarrow's decorative, flat clusters of tiny white flower heads and lacy, dark green leaves are a familiar sight in Boston lots and grassy fields, as they are in sunny meadows, lawns, pastures and waste places throughout much of the world. As perennials, the plants spread by seeds and horizontal rootstocks. The first year plants, evident as low rosettes of lacy, fernlike leaves, are perhaps as familiar as the mature ones.

Yarrow is an herb of ancient medicinal repute. It reportedly has been used for stopping bleeding and healing wounds, and for relieving inflammations and toothache, and even for preventing baldness. According to legend, its powers to heal were first discovered by Achilles, who used it on his soldiers' wounds in the Trojan War.

Yarrow was grown in Colonial days as a medicinal herb, and it is lovely enough to be included still in purely decorative flower gardens today. It has been grown with Thyme, Clover, and Camomile in mixed lawns in Europe, as it is more drought resistant than grasses, and its rich color and dense texture contribute to the appearance of such lawns.

Sunflower Family (Compositae)

18

Sweet Clover — *Melilotus alba*

Naturalized from Europe

HEIGHT: up to 6 feet.

LEAVES: dark green, divided into 3 narrow leaflets ½-2 inches long.

FLOWERS: fragrant, white, ⅛-¼ inch long, in narrow, slightly curving spikes. June to October.

This tall, bushy plant is one of the largest herbaceous weeds growing in Boston lots. It is common on porous soil throughout the United States and sometimes is cultivated as a "green manure" or cover crop, as is the Red Clover.

Sweet Clover's popular name is derived from the honey-like fragrance of its flowers. The flowers are held in distinctive, long, curving spikes which are not conspicuous from a distance, but are attractive at close hand against the rich, dark green of its leaves.

The plant is biennial. It reproduces by seeds which may lie dormant in the soil for many years and germinate when conditions eventually become favorable for growth.

The Yellow Sweet Clover (*Melilotus officinalis*), similar to the above species in most respects other than the color of the flowers, also is found in Boston's lots, but it is much less frequent.

Legume Family (Leguminosae)

20

White Clover — *Trifolium repens*

Naturalized from Europe

HEIGHT: creeping, only a few inches high.

LEAVES: dark green, divided into 3 rounded leaflets ¼-1 inch long.

FLOWERS: white or rose-tinged, in dense, globose clusters ½-1¼ inches across. May to October.

One of the world's most widespread plants, this perennial often forms a beautiful, lush groundcover over the infertile soil of old building lots. Its ability to thrive on poor soil is largely due to its capacity to increase the supply of available nitrogen through the action of nitrogen-fixing bacteria associated with its roots. Since it actually improves the soil it grows on, especially after being turned under, White Clover is sometimes cultivated as a "green manure" or cover crop. In addition, the flowers are attractive to bees and make a very fine honey.

Its delicate, rich green leaves and white or rose-tinted flowers form an attractive, thick, rapidly spreading carpet; a solitary seedling can cover 10 square feet by the end of summer. All the plant seems to require to thrive is well-drained soil.

Legume Family (Leguminosae)

21

Arrowhead — *Sagittaria latifolia*

Native to the United States

HEIGHT: to 2 feet.

LEAVES: to 1 foot long and half as broad.

FLOWERS: about an inch across, with 3 white petals and a yellow center. July to September.

Arrowheads are generally found in shallow water along the edges of lakes, ponds, or sluggish streams. In Boston they are most common in the Fens and along the Muddy River. The broad, arrowhead-shaped leaves originating from the base of the plant, and the dainty white flowers are not likely to be confused with those of any other wild plant in Boston.

In the autumn, Arrowheads produce potato-like tubers, an inch or two in diameter, at the ends of long, underground runners. These are eaten by ducks, muskrats, and other aquatic animals, and they formed an important item in the diets of many of the American Indian tribes. They are evidently quite good, either roasted or boiled.

Water-plantain Family (Alismataceae)

22

Galinsoga — *Galinsoga ciliata*

Naturalized from Tropical America

HEIGHT: to a foot, but usually shorter.

LEAVES: dull green, hairy, 1-3 inches long.

FLOWERS: in small, inconspicuous heads, about ¼ inch broad, with 5 short, white "petals" and a dirty-yellowish center. June to November.

A rather undistinguished-looking plant that does not have a local common name, Galinsoga is one of the very few weeds in our area that originated in Tropical America. It arrived in New England in the mid-1800's and is now widespread, being particularly abundant in gardens or other recently-cultivated soil. It has also appeared in several European countries.

Galinsoga is an annual, and produces seeds prolifically. The seeds attach easily onto clothing, doubtless aiding in dispersal of the plant.

Sunflower Family (Compositae)

23

Chickweed — *Stellaria media*

Naturalized from Europe

HEIGHT: more or less prostrate.

LEAVES: ½-1½ inches long.

FLOWERS: tiny white, ¼ inch across. February to December.

   This rather fragile-looking plant is distinguished by its striking success throughout the world; it may be the most common weed on earth. It appeared in New England shortly after the first settlers arrived from Europe, and it now is established in lawns and grass-land and the cultivated soils of gardens and fields throughout the United States. While it can grow in a wide variety of habitats, it is most aggressive when growing on rich, moist soil.
   Part of Chickweed's success in spreading is due to its capacity to begin producing seeds — and hence a new generation — in little more than a month after its seeds have germinated. In addition, the blooming season is very long; in favorable spots the plant may bloom through the winter.
   Despite its annoying aggression, Chickweed has useful features. Its young shoots may be eaten in salads or cooked as a vegetable, and its seeds are eaten by birds.

Pink Family (Caryophyllaceae)

24

White Campion — *Lychnis alba*

Naturalized from Europe

HEIGHT: up to 3 feet.

LEAVES: 1-3 inches long, slender, hairy.

FLOWERS: white or pale pink, 1 inch across, fragrant. June to August.

    In midsummer this plant is often found blooming in open, grassy lots in Boston. The lovely, fragile flowers usually open in the evening and are closed by early the next day. They are pollinated by night-flying moths which are attracted by their fragrance and pale color.

    White Campion grows most abundantly on rich, well-drained soil. It is common locally along roadsides and in grassland in the eastern, north-central and northwestern states. It is often seen in new seedings of grass, clover or alfalfa, for its seeds are abundantly produced and are a common impurity among the commercially available seeds of such plants. White Campion also spreads by forming new shoots along its underground rootstock.

Pink Family (Caryophyllaceae)

25

Bladder Campion — *Silene cucubalus*

Naturalized from Europe

HEIGHT: up to 2 feet.

LEAVES: 1-3 inches long, smooth, gray-green.

FLOWERS: white, ½ inch across. June to September.

The smooth, gray-green stems and leaves of this delicate perennial easily distinguish it from the hairy White Campion (*Lychnis alba*), which has a similar flower.

Bladder Campion came to the United States from Europe. It spreads both by seeds and creeping perennial rootstocks, and it is often encountered in fields, meadows, and along roadsides in the northeastern states. It also is seen locally in the Pacific Northwest.

Pink Family (Caryophyllaceae)

Ox-eye Daisy — *Chrysanthemum leucanthemum*

Naturalized from Europe

HEIGHT: up to 1-2 feet.

LEAVES: lower leaves 2-4 inches long, clustered into a low rosette; upper leaves narrower and clasping.

FLOWERS: large flowerheads 1-2 inches across, with white rays and a conspicuous yellow center. June to July.

Its bright flowers make an occasional conspicuous appearance in sunny fields and old building lots in Boston, but the Ox-eye Daisy does not grow as abundantly in Boston soil as one would expect from its performance in old fields, meadows, pastures and roadsides of more rural areas. It came to the United States with early settlers, and its presence in New England was noted by the seventeenth century. Today this plant has spread throughout most parts of the country. Its seed production is abundant, and the seeds may lie buried for years yet still germinate. They also may pass unharmed through the digestive systems of animals, aiding in the plant's persistence and spread on grazing land.

Ox-eye Daisy has a history of medicinal use since classical times. The entire plant was used in a tea which was reputed to act as an anti-spasmodic, helpful for treating asthma, whooping cough and nerves.

The leaves of this plant have a tangy taste and are occasionally used in salads.

Sunflower Family (Compositae)

Asters — *Aster* spp.

Native to the United States   A. ericoides

HEIGHT: 6 inches-3 feet.

LEAVES: variable among the different species, from narrow and grass-like to broad and heart-shaped, usually with toothed edges.

FLOWERS: daisy-like heads ¼-1½ inches broad, with white, pink, or purple rays and a yellow or purplish center. August to November.

Along with the Goldenrods, Asters are among the most conspicuous late summer and fall-flowering plants in many parts of the United States. Many species, most of them native perennials, are found in a wide variety of habitats from rich woods to dry roadsides. Some of the species are attractive enough to be cultivated in gardens, but they are less commonly grown in this country than in England, where they, or their hybrids, are known as Michaelmas Daisies.

Several species are found in Boston. Perhaps the most common is the Heath Aster (*Aster ericoides*), a weedy plant with long arching branches nearly covered with small white heads in season. The Heart-leaved Aster (*Aster divaricatus*), with few, relatively large, white heads per plant, is occasional in wooded areas of the Fens and along the Muddy River. Several species with purple flowers sometimes are encountered in a variety of habitats, from wet areas to dry, sunny lots.

Sunflower Family (Compositae)

28

Daisy Fleabane — *Erigeron annuus*

Native to the United States

HEIGHT: 1-2 feet.

LEAVES: hairy, coarsely-toothed, the lower ones to 6 inches long, the stem leaves shorter.

FLOWERS: daisy-like heads about ½ inch across with many, slender white to pink rays and a yellow center. June to September.

This rather coarse annual weed is found in many parts of the world, but it is a native in this country. It is a particular pest in hayfields across the United States, and seed-bearing plants are often transported in bales of hay. The seeds are a common impurity of grass seed. In Boston it is most common in sunny, grassy lots.

The flower heads of Daisy Fleabane are quite attractive. They are similar to those of many of our Asters, but the plants should not be confused since Asters generally bloom late in the season. The leaves of this or related species, when dried and made into a powder, were supposedly good for getting rid of fleas; hence the common name "Fleabane."

Sunflower Family (Compositae)

29

Japanese Knotweed — *Polygonum cuspidatum*

Naturalized from Japan

HEIGHT: up to 8 feet.

LEAVES: dark green, 3-6 inches long.

FLOWERS: small, creamy-white, in showy clusters about 4-5 inches long. August to September.

This is a striking plant when it is in full bloom in late summer. But under the frothy cascade of flowers lies an amazingly aggressive plant. It spreads rapidly from long underground rhizomes, forming large clumps which are difficult to eradicate; the shoots are even capable of emerging through a layer of asphalt.

Japanese Knotweed was originally introduced into the United States as an exotic garden plant, but it has escaped from cultivation and has spread aggressively throughout the northeastern region. In Boston it grows abundantly in rather rich, damp soil, such as that of parks and gardens, and it is particularly well-established along the moist banks of the Muddy River.

Cooked for a few minutes, its young stems (up to 1 foot long) are edible and apparently quite delicious.

Buckwheat Family (Polygonaceae)

Hollyhock — *Althaea rosea*

Escaped from cultivation

HEIGHT: 4-8 feet.

LEAVES: roundish, but with a scalloped or lobed margin, to 10 inches broad, with a long stalk.

FLOWERS: showy, 3-4 inches broad, with 5 pink or white petals. July to September.

Hollyhocks are among the few of our garden plants that have become established in the wild in Boston. We have seen them in a number of locations, and they seem to do well even in grassy lots.

Hollyhocks are native to China, but they were cultivated in England as early as 1593. They were grown in this country before 1700. Many garden forms have appeared, with single or double flowers from white through yellow to pink and red. However, as is the case with many garden plants, only those forms resembling the wild plants do well as escapes; wild forms of Hollyhocks have white or pink, single flowers.

Mallow Family (Malvaceae)

31

P. punctatum

P. persicaria

P. lapathifolium

32

Smartweeds — *Polygonum* spp.

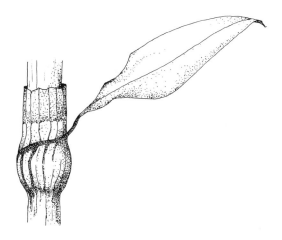

Detail of a node

Some introduced from Europe; others native to the United States

HEIGHT: up to 2 feet, erect or sprawling.

LEAVES: 1-8 inches long, often marked by a brown blotch near the center.

FLOWERS: small, white or pink, in usually dense, erect or drooping spikes ½-3 inches long. May to October.

One of the several species of Smartweed can be found growing in most every situation in Boston, from unweeded planters and sidewalk cracks to vacant lots. Almost all are annual weeds, and their seeds are eaten and dispersed by birds. Smartweeds are members of the Knotweed group, and although they are different in appearance from the others already discussed, they all share one common characteristic: the nodes of the stem (where the leaves are attached) are swollen and surrounded by a papery sheath, resembling knots on a string. This is the origin of the common name, "Knotweed."

A few species of Smartweed have leaves with a brown blotch, resembling a thumbprint, near the center. These sometimes are called "Lady's Thumb."

Buckwheat Family (Polygonaceae)

33

Bouncing Bet — *Saponaria officinalis*

Naturalized from Europe

HEIGHT: up to 2 feet.

LEAVES: 1-3 inches long.

FLOWERS: to 1 inch across, fragrant, pink. July to September.

Throughout the summer the flowers of this ornamental perennial are conspicuous along fences, walls, garden edges and in old vacant lots in Boston.

Bouncing Bet arrived in New England with settlers from Europe in the seventeenth century. It has spread aggressively by seeds and perennial rootstocks, and today it is found in damp soil along roadsides and railroad tracks, and in old fields and pastures throughout the eastern United States. A double-flowered form is more common than the single-flowered in many areas but we did not see it in Boston.

Bruised in water, the stems and leaves of Bouncing Bet emit a juice which makes a lather once considered an excellent substitute for soap in cleaning particularly delicate fabrics and china. The plant also has been used as an antiseptic for treating wounds, and it has a reputation for being effective in relieving the itching of Poison Ivy.

Pink Family (Caryophyllaceae)

Common Milkweed — *Asclepias syriaca*

Native to the United States

HEIGHT: 2-5 feet.

LEAVES: 4-9 inches long, pale and downy on the underside.

FLOWERS: dull pinkish-purple, in rounded clusters 2-3 inches across, fragrant. June to August.

The Milkweed's plumed seeds are its trademark. In September when the ripe pods split open, masses of light, silky seeds take to the air, floating on the slightest breeze.

Milkweed forms large colonies in rich gravelly soil in old fields and waste places of the eastern United States. Usually it is found growing in patches, because the plant is perennial and spreads not only by seeds but also by horizontal root-stocks, along which new plants arise.

The tender young shoots, leaves, and even flower buds and seed pods of Milkweed are edible, and provide good greens if their bitterness is removed in several changes of water during cooking. Indians used its roots, juices, and seeds medicinally, and made string and rope out of its fibers. Although Common Milkweed is perhaps too invasive a grower to be recommended for gardens, the flowers are attractive and sweet-scented.

Milkweed Family (Asclepiadaceae)

36

Red Clover — *Trifolium pratense*

Naturalized from Europe

HEIGHT: up to 2 feet.

LEAVES: divided into 3 rounded leaflets 1¼-2½ inches long, each marked by a distinctive light band.

FLOWERS: pink to magenta, in dense globose clusters, 1-1½ inches across. May to October.

This plant grows in lush clumps on the poor soil of old building lots. Like White Clover, Vetch and other leguminous plants, it is sometimes cultivated as a "green manure" or cover crop.

Red Clover is easily distinguished from other Clovers by its large pink or magenta-colored flower clusters and the distinctive light bands which appear on each leaflet. It came to North America shortly after the first settlers arrived from Europe. It may have been introduced intentionally as a cover crop, since it was highly thought of by the English as a soil conditioner.

Legume Family (Leguminosae)

37

Nightshade — *Solanum* spp.

S. dulcamara

Naturalized from Europe

Two nightshades are encountered in Boston. The annual Black Nightshade (*Solanum nigrum*) is distinguished by its white flowers and small, shiny black berries, and it is partial to fields and shady sites. The perennial Deadly Nightshade (*Solanum dulcamara*) is an herbaceous vine which favors rich, damp soil, and bears violet-blue flowers and shiny red berries.

The berries of both plants are poisonous, causing extreme nausea and cramps if eaten. However, the severity of their effects seems to vary considerably. The berries of Black Nightshade have been used in baking, but it would seem wisest not to eat any part of either plant.

Nightshade Family (Solanaceae)

Vetch — *Vicia cracca*

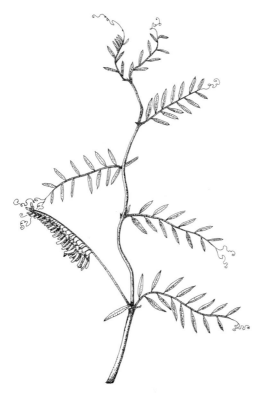

Naturalized from Europe

HEIGHT: climbing or trailing stems,
1-3 feet long.

LEAVES: rows of tiny, narrow leaflets ½-1 inch long.

FLOWERS: blue-purple, 1 inch long.
June to August.

This plant has an interesting mechanical method of seed dispersal, similar to that of the Yellow Wood Sorrel and Jewelweed:
when its ripe seed pods slit open, the seeds within are flung away
from the parent plant.

Vetch has been cultivated in fields as a cover crop or "green
manure" and sometimes as a forage plant. It also has been used on
highway embankments and roadsides as a rapid-growing ground
cover.

Legume Family (Leguminosae)

39

Burdock — *Arctium minus*

Naturalized from Europe

HEIGHT: up to 3-4 feet.

LEAVES: 10-18 inches long, about half as broad.

FLOWERS: pink, or occasionally purple, in dense, thistle-like flower heads ½ inch across. July to October.

Inadvertently carried from Europe to the United States by early settlers, Burdock was already recorded in New England by the seventeenth century. Today it is widespread on rich soil in waste places and neglected farm yards throughout the United States, and its large, rather dull, green leaves are conspicuous in many Boston lots.

During the first year of growth, a distinctive 1-2 foot rosette of large leaves and a thick taproot are produced, followed the second year by a flowering stalk which reaches 3 to 4 feet in height. After flowering and producing the familiar prickly burrs which cling to the coats of passing animals and humans, each plant usually dies, for the Burdock is a biennial.

The first-year roots, young leaves and peeled young flower stalks all are edible, and Burdock has been so valued as a food plant in Japan that a special garden variety has been developed. The plant has been used medicinally since ancient times. It was believed that its roots would draw out the poison of vipers, or cure eczema and toothache.

Sunflower Family (Compositae)

Bull-thistle — *Cirsium vulgare*

Naturalized from Europe

HEIGHT: 3-6 feet.

LEAVES: coarsely and irregularly lobed, the teeth tipped with sharp spines; lower leaves to a foot or more long, the upper ones smaller.

FLOWERS: medium purple, in heads 1-3 inches broad and very prickly at the base. June to September.

Anyone who has tried to get close enough to a Bull-thistle to admire its attractive flower heads, let alone pick them, is well aware of the vicious spines so characteristic of the stems and leaves of this plant. It is conspicuous in pastures, fields, roadsides and other open places throughout the United States. Being a biennial, a first year plant appears as a broad rosette of spiny leaves. Flowering occurs the second year, and then the plant dies. The seed head resembles that of a Dandelion, only denser and much larger, and the light seeds are dispersed by the wind.

Sunflower Family (Compositae)

42

Purple Loosestrife — *Lythrum salicaria*

Naturalized from Europe

HEIGHT: 3-6 feet.

LEAVES: slender, 2-5 inches long.

FLOWERS: magenta, about ½ inch across, in dense, slender spikes. July to August.

This very showy plant is abundant in marshy or other wet places throughout the northeastern United States. In mid- to late summer it turns acres of such areas into sheets of magenta. It is particularly conspicuous along Route 1 in Dedham and along Route 128 south of Boston. Although most characteristic of wet areas, it does appear here and there in dry lots in Boston, but usually only in scattered instances.

A native of Europe, Purple Loosestrife is gradually extending its range in North America. This perennial produces large quantities of light, easily windblown seeds. It has become rather a serious pest in New England because it chokes out the native vegetation in places where it has become established.

Loosestrife Family (Lythraceae)

43

Viper's Bugloss — *Echium vulgare*

Naturalized from Europe

HEIGHT: 1-2½ feet.

LEAVES: 2-6 inches long, hairy.

FLOWERS: bright blue, ½-1 inch long, in short curving clusters on a loose spike. June to July.

In Boston the lovely bright blue funnel-shaped blossoms of Viper's Bugloss are a welcome sight when they appear in early summer, but in the fields and pastures of more rural areas this plant can be a persistent and troublesome weed. It is so despised in Australia that it is known as "Paterson's Curse," after the unfortunate settler who introduced it to that country.

Viper's Bugloss arrived in New England from Europe by the seventeenth century. Today it is widespread in dry, gravelly fields, meadows and roadsides throughout the eastern United States.

A biennial, this plant produces a stout taproot and rosette of leaves in the first year, followed by a flowering stalk the next. Viper's Bugloss is a difficult plant to eradicate because it easily regenerates if any portion of the deep taproot is left in the ground.

Viper's Bugloss was reputed to be effective against poisonous snake bites, either made into a drink, or chewed and laid directly on the bite.

Borage Family (Boraginaceae)

Chicory — *Cichorium intybus*

Naturalized from Europe

HEIGHT: 1½-5 feet.

LEAVES: lower leaves 4-8 inches long, clustered in a flat, evergreen rosette; upper leaves small and clasping.

FLOWERS: Bright blue, or rarely pink or white, daisy-like flowerheads, 1-1½ inches across. June to August.

In midsummer Chicory's distinctive blue, daisy-like flowers and stiff, almost leafless stems are conspicuous in Boston's fields and old building lots.

Chicory was originally brought to the United States by early settlers, who cultivated it in their gardens as a food plant. Today it ranges through old fields and roadsides in most parts of the country. It is particularly persistent in light, sandy, somewhat alkaline soil.

Chicory has long been a popular vegetable and salad plant. Its large basal leaves are cooked for greens, or blanched and used in salads. Its roots are boiled and served with butter, or roasted and used as a coffee substitute or additive. The plant also has been used medicinally for several disorders. It was said to be useful for jaundice and to be comforting for a weak stomach.

Sunflower Family (Compositae)

45

Dayflower — *Commelina communis*

Naturalized from Asia

HEIGHT: usually less than a foot; creeping.

LEAVES: smooth and lustrous, 1-2 inches long.

FLOWERS: bright blue, ½ inch across. July to September.

    Since most of the New World's early contacts, both in commerce and immigration, were with Europe, the great majority of its introduced weeds have come from that continent. Asiatic weeds are rare here, but the Dayflower is one which has become well-established. An annual species, it prefers soils richer and moister than those found in most building lots. In Boston, at least, it is most common in gardens.

    The curious flowers, with two of the petals bright blue and conspicuous, and the third one tiny and greenish, open only in bright light. This, plus the fact that they last only a single day, accounts for the plant's common name. The creeping, lustrous green foliage resembles that of the "Wandering Jew," a common house plant and a close relative of the Dayflower.

Spiderwort Family (Commelinaceae)

Yellow Iris — *Iris pseudacorus*

Naturalized from Europe

HEIGHT: 2-4 feet.

LEAVES: very slender, to 3 or rarely 4 feet long and less than 1½ inches broad, gray-green.

FLOWERS: showy, bright yellow, 3 or 4 inches broad. June.

This beautiful plant was brought to America as a garden plant sometime before 1700 and has since escaped to the wild. It is common in wet areas, particularly at the edges of ponds and streams, throughout much of the eastern United States. In Boston it is most abundant in the Fens and along the Charles and Muddy Rivers.

This, and many other species of Iris, grow from thick rhizomes or rootstocks which lie just below the surface of the ground. These rhizomes may cause dermatitis if broken and brought into contact with human skin. The Yellow Iris produces abundant seeds, accounting for its ability to spread rapidly in the wild.

Iris Family (Iridaceae)

47

Buttercups — *Ranunculus* spp.

R. acris

Some native to the United States, others naturalized from Europe.

HEIGHT: to 3 feet.

LEAVES: deeply lobed, often with silvery markings on the upper surface.

FLOWERS: showy, about 1 inch across, with 5 shiny, bright yellow petals. April to August.

Several species of Buttercups are found in Boston, but two in particular, both naturalized from Europe, are common and conspicuous. The Bulbous Buttercup (*Ranunculus bulbosus*) is a low plant (seldom more than 18 inches tall) that is common in lawns, gardens and other cultivated places as well as in sidewalk cracks. The leaves are often silver-spotted on their upper surface. The Common Buttercup (*Ranunculus acris*) is a taller plant, often nearly a yard tall, that is most common in grassy lots.

The stems and leaves of these perennials contain a substance which may irritate the mouth and stomach if eaten or cause blisters if rubbed on the skin. Cattle have died from eating them in quantity.

The Celandine (*Chelidonium majus*) is often mistaken for a Buttercup. The flowers of this plant, however, have only 4 petals, and they are dull-textured rather than shiny.

Crowfoot Family
  (Ranunculaceae)

R. bulbosus

Celandine — *Chelidonium majus*

Naturalized from Europe

HEIGHT: up to 2-3 feet.

LEAVES: green with grayish undersides, irregularly cut into 5 parts.

FLOWERS: bright yellow, ½ inch across. May to July.

The delicate, scalloped leaves and bright yellow flowers of Celandine are conspicuous along the rich, damp edges of Boston gardens. This plant was originally brought to the United States by New England settlers who valued it as a medicinal herb and grew it in their gardens. Today, it has spread to rich soil in farmyards, roadsides, gardens and woodland edges from the northeastern United States south to Georgia, Tennessee and Missouri.

A biennial, Celandine lives for two years only. In the first year of growth low tufts of foliage are produced, followed in the second year by the lovely flowering stalks.

The roots and yellow juice of Celandine have been said to cure a variety of ailments, ranging from ringworm and warts to "the itch." The juice, however, may produce skin irritation.

Poppy Family (Papaveraceae)

50

Yellow Wood Sorrel — *Oxalis stricta*

Native to the United States

HEIGHT: up to 10 inches, but most often low and somewhat creeping.

LEAVES: clover-like, separated into 3 leaflets, each to ½ inch across.

FLOWERS: yellow, ¼-½ inch across. May to September.

    This plant is often mistaken for clover since its leaves are so similar in shape, but its small, five-petaled yellow flowers are distinctive.

    In appearance, at least, Wood Sorrel is a rather charming plant. Close relatives with larger flowers are considered decorative enough to be cultivated in gardens and on windowsills. It is a native of the United States, and is often encountered in woods and dry fields throughout the country, but it grows most abundantly in the eastern states. Rather than thriving in the rigorous environment of most building lots, in Boston it is usually found growing in or near gardens where it is often quite a persistent weed.

    Wood Sorrel has an interesting method of avoiding competition between the parent plant and its offspring. When a ripe pod splits open, its interior lining turns completely inside out, and thus explosively catapults the seeds some distance away.

    Its foliage is rich in vitamin C and is sometimes used in salads; however, it should not be eaten in large quantities as the plant also has a high oxalic acid content and could be toxic.

Wood Sorrel Family (Oxalidaceae)

52

Purslane — *Portulaca oleracea*

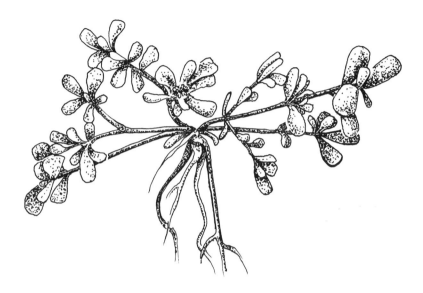

Naturalized from Europe

HEIGHT: sprawling, fleshy stems, up to 12 inches long.

LEAVES: fleshy, often tinged reddish, ½-1½ inches long.

FLOWERS: inconspicuous, pale yellow, ¼ inch across, opening only in bright sunlight. July to September.

Purslane grows almost all over the world. It is a hot weather plant, springing up on bare soil in local fields and gardens from June onward. It grows only on cultivated soil, and is often very difficult to eradicate.

Purslane is an excellent and well-respected food plant which has been encouraged and cultivated since ancient times. The tips of its succulent young stems can be harvested periodically throughout the summer and cooked and seasoned like Spinach, or eaten raw in salads.

Other members of this genus are cultivated in gardens for their decorative flowers.

Purslane Family (Portulacaceae)

53

St. John's-wort — *Hypericum perforatum*

Naturalized from Europe

HEIGHT: 1-3 feet.

LEAVES: ½-1 inch long, pale green.

FLOWERS: golden yellow, ¾-1 inch broad, in clusters. July and August.

In midsummer, clusters of the bright, golden-yellow flowers of St. John's-wort make a conspicuous appearance in grassy fields and old building lots in Boston.

This familiar perennial has a wide distribution throughout many parts of the world. Its seeds are a common impurity in grass seed, and have been most likely scattered from one part of the world to another in shipments of hay. This plant came to New England with the early settlers, and has since spread through much of temperate North America. It prospers on dry, gravelly soil, and it is a difficult plant to suppress, for it spreads vigorously from short runners. It also produces seeds prolifically, perhaps as many as 30,000 per plant in a single season. The seeds are easily carried off by the wind, and they are so light that St. John's-wort even has been found growing in the steeples of old churches.

St. John's-wort was listed in the early herbals as useful to stop bleeding, cure burns, heal ulcers, or as a laxative. A bit of the plant was supposed to provide protection against witchcraft and enchantment; also damage from storms, thunder, and evil spirits. It also has been used as a yellow dye for wool.

St. John's-wort Family
(Hypericaceae)

54

Winter Cress — *Barbarea* spp.

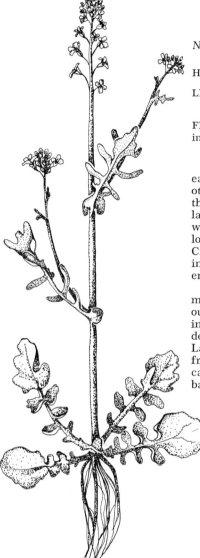

Naturalized from Europe

HEIGHT: to 2 feet tall.

LEAVES: deep glossy green, deeply lobed, 2-6 inches long.

FLOWERS: bright yellow, about ¼ inch across.

Throughout many parts of the eastern United States, these and other yellow-flowered members of the Mustard family are particularly conspicuous in the spring when they turn fallow fields yellow with their blooms. Winter Cress is not particularly common in Boston, but it is occasionally encountered in open, sunny lots.

The leaves of Winter Cress remain green and succulent throughout the winter and, when boiled in two changes of water, are evidently quite good as greens. The Latin name *Barbarea* was derived from the fact that these plants can be eaten as early as St. Barbara's Day in early December.

Mustard Family (Cruciferae)

55

Butter and Eggs — *Linaria vulgaris*

Naturalized from Europe

HEIGHT: up to 1-2 feet.

LEAVES: 1-2 inches long, about ⅛ inch wide; gray-green.

FLOWERS: pale yellow and orange; about 1 inch long. June to October.

The delicate yellow and orange Snapdragon-like flowers and the narrow gray-green foliage of this rugged perennial appear in sidewalk crevices and open, sunny lots throughout Boston. Butter and Eggs was introduced to New England by the seventeenth century. Today it grows profusely along roadsides and waste places throughout much of the United States. While seed production is apt to be poor without cross-pollination, the shoot production of this plant is abundant: over one hundred shoots may be produced by a typical two-year-old plant!

Butter and Eggs derives its popular name from the color of its flowers: butter yellow with a blotch nearly the color of the yolk of a fresh egg.

The early herbalists listed this plant as useful in treating a variety of disorders, ranging from skin eruptions to jaundice and ulcers.

Figwort Family
(Scrophulariaceae)

56

Mullein — *Verbascum thapsus*

Naturalized from Europe

HEIGHT: up to 7 feet.

LEAVES: light green, woolly; lower leaves 4-12 inches long, in a rosette 8-24 inches across; upper leaves smaller.

FLOWERS: bright sulphur yellow, ½ inch across in a narrow dense cylindrical spike, but only a few open at any given time. June to September.

Even from quite a distance one can easily spot Mullein's rosette of large, soft, fuzzy, pale green leaves, and its thin, cylindrical flower spike, which often reaches up to 7 feet or so in height.

This biennial produces massive amounts of seeds, but it is not an invasive plant, and it cannot tolerate crowding. It grows on dry, stony soils in old fields and meadows and along roadsides throughout the United States. It may have been intentionally imported into New England as a garden plant, for it has a long reputation as a good medicinal herb.

Mullein has been found useful for quite a variety of other purposes as well. Over the years its leaves have provided a soft lining in shoes; dried and floated in oil, they are serviceable lamp wicks. Its long stalks have been coated with fat to serve as tall candles.

Figwort Family
(Scrophulariaceae)

Evening Primrose — *Oenothera biennis*

Native to the United States

HEIGHT: 2-6 feet, with reddish stems.

LEAVES: 3-6 inches long, hairy.

FLOWERS: pale yellow, about 1 inch across, fragrant. June to September.

The Evening Primrose is one of our native weeds, and it is a common plant of fields and roadsides throughout the eastern and central United States. During the summer it occasionally forms large colonies on dry, sunny sites in Boston.

This plant is distinguished by its tall, erect, reddish stems and its pale yellow flowers. Its blossoms usually open at dusk, when they emit a soft fragrance, and close by early the next day; thus, the origin of the common name.

Being biennials, the first year plants appear merely as rosettes of rough-hairy leaves. At this stage, the thick, fleshy taproots are palatable, if cooked in two changes of water and if collected at the right time during the winter months. Otherwise they are too peppery to appeal to most people.

Evening Primrose Family
(Onagraceae)

58

Goldenrods — *Solidago* spp.

Native to the United States

HEIGHT: 1-5 feet.

LEAVES: variable among the different species, from narrow and grass-like to 3 inches broad, starting in a basal rosette.

FLOWERS: yellow heads ⅛-¼ inch broad, in slender, pyramidal, or flat clusters. August to October.

From late summer until frost, the bright yellow flowers of Goldenrod are conspicuous in all sorts of habitats across the country, particularly in the eastern half. There are many different species, and even a botanist often has trouble identifying them. Several species are found in grassy fields and lots in Boston, but the Canada Goldenrod (*Solidago canadensis*), pictured here, is perhaps the most common.

Although generally thought of as a major cause of hay fever, most species of Goldenrod shed pollen in quantities too small to be significant. This erroneous notion probably arose because of the fact that these are among the most conspicuous plants during one of the worst hay fever seasons.

Sunflower Family (Compositae)

59

Sow Thistles — *Sonchus* spp.

Naturalized from Europe

HEIGHT: to 6 feet tall.

LEAVES: coarsely and irregularly lobed, the lower ones to a foot or more long, the upper ones smaller.

FLOWERS: yellow, Dandelion-like heads, 1-2 inches across; followed by fluffy seed heads, again like those of Dandelions. June to September.

Several species of Sow Thistle are found in grassy or gravelly lots in Boston, and we will make no attempt here to separate them. They all are coarse herbs that resemble the Wild Lettuce in many respects, including the presence of a milky juice in all parts of the plant. The flowers of the Sow Thistles are larger, however, and the leaves have spiny teeth all along their edges. These spiny teeth resemble those of Thistles, but are not so stiff.

Most of these plants are annuals, but the Field Sow Thistle (*Sonchus arvensis*), is a perennial, and it spreads vigorously by a fast-growing underground rootstock. The leaves of the Common Sow Thistle (*Sonchus oleraceus*) are cooked as greens in Europe.

Sunflower Family (*Compositae*)

S. oleraceus

60

Wild Lettuce — *Lactuca scariola*

Naturalized from Europe

HEIGHT: 1-5 feet.

LEAVES: pale green, to 6 inches long, with a row of sharp prickles along the midvein on the under-side.

FLOWERS: numerous yellow, Dandelion-like heads (only a few open at any one time) ¼-½ inch across; followed by fluffy seed heads, again resembling those of Dandelions. July to October.

Although this plant is closely related to the cultivated Lettuce, the similarities are not particularly obvious to the casual observer. The leaves of the two plants are quite different, yet the flowers are nearly identical, although few gardeners ever get to see Lettuce flowers because they harvest the crop before the plants are old enough to produce them.

This coarse annual is common both in cultivated and in uncultivated ground throughout the United States. It is particularly troublesome if abundant in grain fields, because the milky juice present in all parts of the plant can clog threshing machines. The light seeds are dispersed by the wind, and are a common impurity of grain. These factors account for the plant's widespread distribution.

One curious habit of the Wild Lettuce, which may be useful for identification purposes, is that, when it is grown in the open, its leaves are oriented vertically. This is well illustrated in the accompanying photograph. When grown in the shade, the leaves are oriented horizontally as in most other plants.

Sunflower Family (Compositae)

61

Hawkweed — *Hieracium canadense*

Native to eastern United States

HEIGHT: to 5 feet.

LEAVES: hairy, irregularly toothed, dull, dark green; 2-6 inches long.

FLOWERS: bright yellow Dandelion-like heads ½-1½ inches across. August to October.

This attractive perennial is one of the most colorful of the late summer- and fall-flowering plants in Boston. It is most common in shady, wooded areas, where it forms dense stands that are conspicuous even when not in flower. Hawkweed is occasionally found in open, sunny lots, as indicated in the photograph above.

Many introduced species of Hawkweed are common weeds in the United States, but this is the only one that is frequently encountered in Boston. According to legend, hawks used the plants to improve their eyesight, hence the common name of the group.

Sunflower Family (Compositae)

62

Dandelion — *Taraxacum officinale*

Naturalized from Europe

HEIGHT: to 15 inches.

LEAVES: 3-12 inches long, irregularly lobed, in a basal rosette.

FLOWERS: golden-yellow flowerheads to 2 inches broad, opening only in sunny weather and closing at night. Mostly blooms April to June.

This scourge of suburban homeowners is basically a very attractive plant. However, few people stop to appreciate the beauty of the flowers as they are eradicating the plants from their lawns and gardens. The common name is a corruption of the French *dent de lion*, which means "lion's tooth", in reference to the plant's jaggedly toothed leaves.

The first Dandelions appeared in New England shortly after the first settlers arrived from Europe. The plant's deep, persistent root and light, widely dispersed seeds have helped it become established in fields, lawns, sidewalk cracks, and roadsides throughout the United States.

The Dandelion is a plant of many uses. Before a plant has flowered, the leaves are excellent, either raw in salads, or cooked like Spinach. Its flowers are used to make wine, and its roots and leaves are used to prepare a medicinal tea.

Sunflower Family (Compositae)

63

Black-eyed Susan — *Rudbeckia hirta*

Native to the United States

HEIGHT: up to 3 feet.

LEAVES: 2-6 inches long, hairy.

FLOWERS: orange-yellow flowerheads 2-4 inches across, with a dark pur-plish-brown center. June to August.

Travelling eastward in shipments of commercial seeds and hay, this striking native of the western prairies has gradually spread to New England fields, meadows and roadsides. It is now so well-established here that, like Queen Anne's Lace, it often is con-sidered to be a native wildflower.

Its large, golden-yellow, daisy-like flowerheads with their dark purplish-brown centers are so attractive that Black-eyed Susan is often cultivated in gardens.

In the first year of growth this biennial appears as a rosette of slender, hairy, green leaves. The second year, showy flowering stalks appear and, after producing seeds, the plant dies.

Sunflower Family (Compositae)

64

Tansy — *Tanacetum vulgare*

Naturalized from Europe

HEIGHT: up to 3 feet.

LEAVES: up to 1 foot long, deep green, fernlike, extremely aromatic.

FLOWERS: golden-yellow, button-like heads ¼-½ inch across or less, in flat-topped clusters. July to September.

Tansy is one of the most appealing of the very common weeds in Boston. Its aromatic, rich green foliage, and its midsummer clusters of distinctive, golden flowers form a splendid cover for the dry, gravelly soil of many old building lots.

Tansy was brought to the United States from Europe as a garden plant, grown for its decorative qualities and its supposed medicinal uses. It has been used in quite a variety of ways: to preserve meat and corpses; to repel insects; as a tea to dispel worms and relieve nausea; and in poultices to relieve rheumatism and gout. Its leaves also are used occasionally in salads as a flavoring.

It is a perennial weed and often grows in dense colonies formed by its creeping rootstocks.

Sunflower Family (Compositae)

66

Jewelweed, Touch-me-not — *Impatiens capensis*

Native to northeastern United States

HEIGHT: 1½-5 feet.

LEAVES: 2-5 inches long, bluish-green.

FLOWERS: orange, or occasionally yellow, speckled with brown or crimson, 1 inch long. June to September

The delicate orange (or yellow) flowers and bluish-green leaves of this lovely New England native are conspicuous in a few damp places in Boston, particularly along the unmowed banks of the Muddy River.

One of the popular names of this plant — "Touch-me-not" — alludes to the sudden way in which its ripe seed capsules burst when they are touched, flinging the seeds to distances of 6 feet or so. The seeds float and are often carried to new locations by running water.

According to tradition, the juice of Jewelweed brings immediate relief from the itching of Poison Ivy and Nettles.

Balsam Family (Balsaminaceae)

67

Pineapple Weed — *Matricaria matricarioides*

Native to western United States

HEIGHT: 3-12 inches.

LEAVES: to 2 inches long with a delicate, fernlike texture, and a scent resembling pineapples.

FLOWERS: inconspicuous, greenish-yellow, in dense flowerheads ¼-½ inch across. May to September.

A rugged, low-growing little annual with aromatic leaves, this plant has spread from its native habitat on the Pacific Coast to old fields and roadsides in the eastern states and on to Europe. It is capable of growing on extremely poor, packed down soil, and is often seen in Boston growing on sites such as dirt paths and the bare patches of playing fields.

Sunflower Family (Compositae)

Beggar-ticks — *Bidens frondosa*

Native to the United States

HEIGHT: up to 5 feet.

LEAVES: 2-5 inches long, dull, dark green leaflets, 3 to 5 per leaf.

FLOWERS: inconspicuous, dull orange-yellow, in heads ½ inch across. August to September.

A tall, drab-looking plant with purplish stems and dull green leaves, Beggar-ticks seems to prosper particularly in the moist soil of Boston gardens, although it does appear even on our driest lots.

Beggar-ticks is native to the United States, and is common in pastures, roadsides, gardens, cultivated fields and waste places across the country. Its seeds are widely distributed, because they are armed with two barbed projections which catch easily on fur and clothing, thus the origin of the generic name *"Bidens"*, meaning "two teeth."

Sunflower Family (Compositae)

69

Ragweed — *Ambrosia artemisiifolia*

Native to the United States

HEIGHT: 1-4 feet.

LEAVES: 2-4 inches long, with a lacy texture.

FLOWERS: inconspicuous, yellowish-green, in dense slender spikes 2-3 inches long. August to September.

An infamous cause of hay fever when its pollen is in the air in late summer, Ragweed is probably one of the most widely detested weeds growing in the United States. It is common to cultivated fields, meadows, pastures and waste places throughout the United States, but it is particularly abundant in the eastern and north central states. Due to its copious seed production and the longevity of its seeds, it is a difficult plant to eradicate once it has been allowed to flower.

While Ragweed does grow on dry, sunny soil in Boston lots, its incidence here is probably greatly overestimated since it closely resembles the more pervasive Mugwort.

Sunflower Family (Compositae)

70

Mugwort — *Artemisia vulgaris*

Naturalized from Europe; possibly native to the western United States as well

HEIGHT: 1-6 feet.

LEAVES: 1-4 inches long, silvery on undersides, strongly aromatic.

FLOWERS: inconspicuous greenish-white heads $\frac{1}{16}$ inch across, in long, slender clusters. July to September.

The coarse reddish stems and lacy foliage of Mugwort are seen practically everywhere in Boston. It seems to thrive in the rubbly soil of old building lots, and its seedlings carpet the ground of these lots in early summer. It has spread across entire blocks in areas of the city where many buildings have been demolished in recent years. Because of its conspicuousness in such areas, Mugwort, probably more than any other weed, signifies municipal neglect to most Bostonians.

This relative of the Sagebrush (*Artemisia tridentata*) is widespread in fields and waste places across the northern and western United States, particularly on limey soil. In appearance, Mugwort, a perennial, so closely resembles the more notorious Ragweed that it is often mistaken for that plant. However, Mugwort is easily distinguished by its strong scent and the silvery undersides of its leaves.

Sunflower Family (Compositae)

71

Horseweed — *Conyza canadensis*

Native to the United States

HEIGHT: to 10 feet, but usually not more than 6 feet.

LEAVES: 1-6 inches long, narrow.

FLOWERS: small, inconspicuous, whitish heads; extremely numerous in a large, branched cluster at the top of the plant. July to October.

This coarse, annual weed is common and conspicuous in old fields, pastures, roadsides, and other open places throughout the United States. In the Southeast, it is the first plant to appear in fallow fields. It is found in a variety of habitats in Boston, but it is mostly abundant in newly cleared lots. Although it may grow to be nearly 10 feet tall, Horseweed often begins to bloom before it has reached a foot in height.

The foliage of Horseweed contains an oil that has been used as a mosquito repellant. This same oil renders the plant unpalatable to grazing animals, and it may produce an irritating reaction on human skin.

Sunflower Family (Compositae)

72

Lamb's Quarters, Pigweed — *Chenopodium album*

Naturalized from Europe

HEIGHT: up to 2-3 feet.

LEAVES: 1-2 inches long, with whitish undersides.

FLOWERS: inconspicuous, greenish, in irregular spikes. June to September.

An ancient and extremely nutritious food plant, Lamb's Quarters was one of the most valued leafy vegetables of early Europeans until Spinach was introduced from Asia in the sixteenth century.

Lamb's Quarters spreads copiously by seeds. It grows abundantly in Boston gardens and lots, and in fields, gardens, pastures and wasteland throughout the United States.

Its succulent young foliage may be cooked for greens, and its seeds can be ground into a flour which resembles buckwheat flour.

Goosefoot Family (Chenopodiaceae)

73

Curly (or Yellow) Dock — *Rumex crispus*

Naturalized from Europe

HEIGHT: up to 3 or 4 feet.

LEAVES: basal leaves 6-12 inches long, upper ones smaller.

FLOWERS: small, greenish, in dense spikes up to 12 inches long. June to September.

    This is one of our most distinctive weeds, for its tall, stiff stalks are topped by large spikes of brown or rusty-colored seeds which stand out conspicuously against the greenness of surrounding vegetation.

    Curly Dock grows in grasslands, old fields, and along roadsides throughout the United States. It appeared in New England shortly after the English arrived. Its perennial roots are deep and persistent, and its seeds are abundantly produced — up to 30,000 have been counted on a single large plant! Its seeds also may lie dormant in the soil for exceptionally long periods of time, allowing future generations of Curly Dock to spring up even after 50 years have passed by.

    Birds are very fond of its seeds, and feed on them throughout the winter. Its thick, yellow roots have been used medicinally, and its first-year rosette of long crinkly leaves are sometimes gathered and cooked like Spinach.

Buckwheat Family (Polygonaceae)

74

Sheep (or Field) Sorrel — *Rumex acetosella*

Naturalized from Europe

HEIGHT: up to 12 inches.

LEAVES: light green, arrow-shaped, ½ to 3 inches.

FLOWERS: very small, greenish or reddish, in spikes. May to September.

This close relative of Curly Dock is distinguished from that plant by its small arrow-shaped leaves and daintier stature, but it too is conspicuous among most surrounding plants, due to its spikes of rusty-colored seeds.

Sheep Sorrel grows on dry, sandy or gravelly soil in old fields and meadows throughout the United States. It can grow on very acid soil where other plants have difficulty, and so it is often associated with such soils, but it also will grow in soils that are more neutral or even slightly alkaline.

This plant appeared in New England shortly after settlers arrived from Europe. Its creeping, perennial rootstocks make it a difficult plant to eradicate.

Sheep Sorrel's leaves have a refreshing, vinegary taste, and they are sometimes eaten raw in salads or cooked like spinach. The substance responsible for the sour taste, however, may be toxic in large quantities.

Buckwheat Family
(Polygonaceae)

75

Plantain — *Plantago* spp.

P. major

P. lanceolata

Some species native to the United States and others naturalized from Europe

The Plantains have a long history as travellers and have kept close company with man. Their association with our paths and roadsides is reflected in their Latin name, *Plantago*, which was derived from a word meaning "footprint."

Three different Plantains are often encountered in Boston. The Narrow-leaved Plantain (*Plantago lanceolata*) has come to us from Europe. It differs from the other species in its narrow leaves and its short flower clusters atop a long slender stalk. It is common in fields, roadsides, and other open areas. The Red-stem Plantain (*Plantago rugellii*), a native plant, and the very similar Broad-leaved Plantain (*Plantago major*), a European plant, both have broad leaves and long, slender flowering and fruiting spikes. They are common in lawns and sidewalk cracks.

The size of these plants varies enormously according to their environments. While all are pesty weeds in grassy places, the Red-stem Plantain has a particularly strong association with roadsides and the packed down soil of yards and paths. All are particularly difficult to eradicate, because they can easily regenerate from their perennial rootstocks if only the tops are chopped off.

Plantain Family (Plantaginaceae)

76

Pokeweed — *Phytolacca americana*

Native to the United States

HEIGHT: up to 8 feet, with reddish stems.

LEAVES: 4-12 inches long.

FLOWERS: small, greenish-white, become purplish with age; in long, slender, drooping clusters. July to August.

This is such a handsome plant that it has been imported to Europe to be grown as an ornamental. In Boston it is most commonly encountered in rather rich, damp ground. The juicy, deep red-purple berries are attractive to birds, which help to disperse the plants, and to children, who may be seriously poisoned by eating them.

All parts of the plants contain poisonous substances. The roots and the area where the roots and stems join are particularly dangerous. The berries reputedly become less toxic with age, and ripe ones have been used in baking, but cases of serious poisoning from eating them indicate that as few as three or four can seriously sicken a child.

The young shoots, however, are considered an excellent substitute for asparagus. If collected when less than 6 inches long, peeled, and boiled in at least two changes of water, they are perfectly safe. Older shoots on mature stems should never be eaten.

Pokeweed Family (Phytolaccaceae)

77

Shepherd's Purse — *Capsella bursa-pastoris*

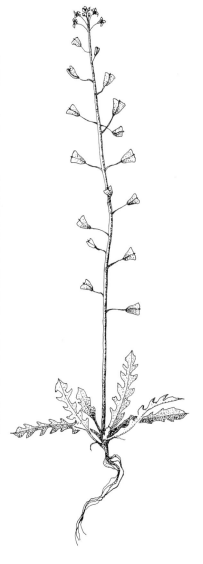

Naturalized from Europe

HEIGHT: 6-18 inches.

LEAVES: lower leaves irregularly toothed or lobed, clustered in a rosette; stem leaves small and clasping.

FLOWERS: tiny, white, inconspicuous $\frac{1}{16}$-$\frac{1}{8}$ inch across. March to December.

The loose spike of tiny, flat, heart-shaped seed pods (resembling shepherd's purses) is the most conspicuous feature of this wiry little annual, which holds the distinction of being one of the most common weeds on earth. Shepherd's Purse grows in all cultivated regions of the world. It reproduces abundantly by seeds and is always assured of a good seed crop because its flowers are self-pollinated before they open. In addition, its seeds are remarkably long-lived and can lie buried in the soil for 35 years or more with occasional germination.

The seeds of Shepherd's Purse are eaten and dispersed by birds. The somewhat peppery young leaves of the plant are edible, and may be used in salads or cooked for greens.

Mustard Family (Cruciferae)

78

Peppergrass — *Lepidium virginicum*

Native to the United States

HEIGHT: 6-24 inches.

LEAVES: lower leaves 1-5 inches long, irregularly lobed; stem leaves smaller, narrower.

FLOWERS: inconspicuous, tiny, greenish-white in slender spikes up to 6 inches long. May to October.

Spikes of tiny, flat, circular seed pods resembling those of Shepherd's Purse are the most distinctive feature of this common little annual, which grows abundantly on most open sites in Boston.

The popular name "Peppergrass" alludes to the peppery taste of the plant's foliage and seeds, both of which are edible and are occasionally used as a minor food. Its young shoots may be substituted for watercress, and its seeds used as a seasoning for salads or soups.

Birds are quite fond of its seeds.

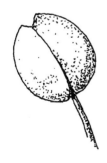

Mustard Family (Cruciferae)

Prostrate Knotweed — *Polygonum aviculare*

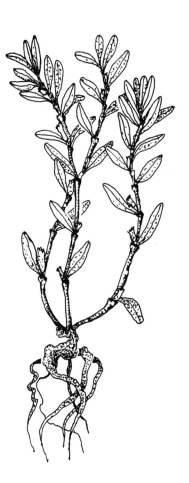

Naturalized from Europe

HEIGHT: prostrate stems, up to 2 feet long.

LEAVES: bluish-green, slender, ¼-1 inch long.

FLOWERS: inconspicuous, greenish-white, tinged with pink ¹⁄₁₂ inch across. June to October.

This species of Knotweed is often encountered on dry, hard-packed ground, and it forms a common ground cover in vacant lots, along the edges of sidewalks, and in garden borders.

An annual weed, its seeds are eaten and dispersed by small birds, and can pass through the digestive tracts undamaged.

Buckwheat Family
(Polygonaceae)

80

Grasses and
Grasslike Plants

Grasses

Grasses are, and have long been, civilized man's most important food plants. The cereal grains — Corn, Wheat, Barley, Rice, Oats, etc. — which feed by far the majority of the world's people as well as their livestock, all are members of this large and widespread plant group.

Many Grasses are low plants with narrow leaves, like the species which commonly make up our lawns. Others, however, such as Corn and the various Bamboos, are much taller with relatively broad leaves. All of them produce small, greenish flowers, arranged in clusters of various types; some dense and spike-like, others loose and airy.

Many different Grasses, including several of the perennial lawn species, are common in a wide variety of habitats in Boston, but only a few of the more readily identifiable ones are included here. Perhaps Boston's most conspicuous Grass, at least by virtue of its size, is the plant known locally as Reed or Bulrush (*Phragmites communis*). Growing to 12 feet tall, this species forms impenetrable thickets along the Muddy River and the waterways in the Fens. This perennial, which spreads rapidly by means of thick, underground stems, is found in wet areas throughout the world. Although considered an unsightly menace by some Bostonians, it has been put to good use by the southwestern Indians as a shaft for arrows and as a weaving material.

Squirrel-tail Grass (*Hordeum jubatum*), a very attractive species, is a relative of the cultivated Barley. A native annual or biennial, it is widespread in North America. The long, tawny bristles that make this plant so conspicuous cause great discomfort to animals if eaten or inhaled. We have seen it only on the waterfront, but it is so conspicuous there that we felt it deserved to be included in this handbook.

Timothy (*Phleum pratense*), a perennial Grass with dense, spike-like flower clusters, is common in older lots in Boston. A native of Europe, it is extensively cultivated because it produces an excellent hay when cured. It has escaped from cultivation and is now a common wild plant in many parts of the United States.

Crab-grasses (*Digitaria* spp.) are persistent weeds on both cultivated and fallow ground in many parts of the world. All are annuals, reproducing by seeds which remain viable for many years after ripening. Although suburban homeowners may despise them as pests in their lawns, some species of Crab-grass make good hay; also the seeds are very nutritious, and in Germany and Poland they are made into a kind of gruel.

Several species of Bent Grass (*Agrostis* spp.) are common weeds in Boston. The flower clusters are large (perhaps as much as a foot tall) and open, composed of many tiny florets on long, thread-like stalks. Large clumps of the Red-top (*Agrostis alba*), one of the most common species, appear as a red haze when fully mature. This species is an important lawn grass.

Grass Family (Gramineae)

82

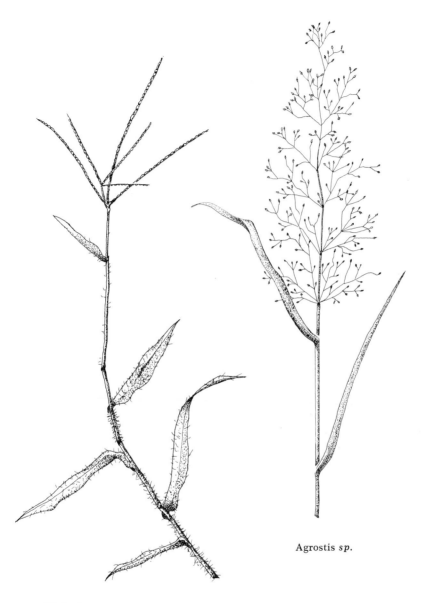

Digitaria *sp.*

Agrostis *sp.*

83

Hordeum jubatum

Phleum pratense

Phragmites communis

85

Sedges

Native to the United States and most other parts of the world

Sedges are a large group of grasslike plants characteristic of moist areas throughout the world, from the tropics to the polar regions. In Boston they grow along waterways or around the small pools which occasionally appear in vacant lots.

Since Sedges are difficult to identify, we have made no attempt here to differentiate between the various types. They resemble Grasses in many ways, and indeed the two groups are closely related. However, Sedges in general have solid stems which are triangular in cross-section, while Grasses have hollow, round stems. In Boston the different species of Sedge vary in height from 3 inches to 5 feet.

Sedges have few economic uses today. They were, and still are, used by the American Indians and native people of other countries for the weaving of baskets and other articles. Papyrus, a kind of Sedge, was used by the ancient Egyptians to make paper.

Sedge Family (Cyperaceae)

87

Cat-tail — *Typha latifolia*

Native to the United States

HEIGHT: up to 6 feet tall.

LEAVES: pale green, very long and slender, only ¼-¾ inch wide, but exceeding the stalk in length.

Cat-tails spring up quickly along the edges of small pools or puddles which occasionally collect in the low areas of old building lots in Boston. They are also to be seen in the Fens, along the Muddy River, and in ditches along local railroad tracks.

The attractive immature fruiting heads, shown in the accompanying illustration, often are used in dried floral arrangements. However, as the heads dry, they tend to come apart in cottony masses. This can be avoided to some extent by applying several coats of hair spray or one of the commercially available acrylic sprays.

Both the young and mature rootstocks may be eaten raw in salads or cooked as a vegetable. While still green, the young flowering spikes may be boiled for a few minutes and then eaten around the tough, central core, like corn on the cob.

Cat-tail Family (Typhaceae)

Trees and Shrubs

Tree of Heaven — *Ailanthus altissima*

Naturalized from Asia

HEIGHT: up to 60 feet or so.

LEAVES: pinnately compound, composed of numerous leaflets 3-7 inches long, with a reddish tinge when they first emerge in the spring.

FLOWERS: greenish-yellow, in clusters. The flowers on male trees have an extremely powerful and unpleasant odor. Showy clusters of red or gold, winged seeds in late summer.

No other tree can compete with the Tree of Heaven in its capacity to make itself at home in the strange environments produced by our cities. It can squeeze up through tiny cracks in a foundation wall or penetrate the mesh of a chain-link fence, and thrive in back alleys, gardens and the harsh, exposed sites of city lots. It seems to grow well regardless of soil moisture and fertility, and its irrepressible vigor and adaptability have allowed it to become a pest where most other trees must be coaxed and coddled to survive.

But if it were not for the spontaneous appearance of this great weed, many sections of cities such as New York and Boston would be far bleaker than they are today, for it is one of the most formidable forces working at bringing shade and greenery into every corner of our urban areas.

The Tree of Heaven was carried from Northern China to England in the mid-eighteenth century, and was brought to the United States by the end of the century. It was widely recommended for city planting at one time, but due to its invasive tendencies it is rarely planted now.

Quassia Family (Simaroubaceae)

Staghorn Sumac — *Rhus typhina*

Native to the central and eastern United States

HEIGHT: to 20 feet, but usually less.

LEAVES: pinnately compound of numerous toothed leaflets 2-4 inches long; smooth, dark green above, pale beneath, turning red in autumn.

FRUIT: erect clusters of hairy, red berries, very showy in late summer.

Staghorn Sumac forms dense, shrubby thickets on the dry, gravelly soil of sunny embankments and vacant lots in Boston. The plants become particularly conspicuous in late summer when the dense, erect clusters of berries, thickly covered with velvety bright red hairs, stand out almost like torches against the surrounding greenery. The thick twigs and branches of Staghorn Sumac also are densely covered with soft hairs, which give them the velvety brown appearance of a stag's immature antlers.

The berries of this Sumac are edible, and a refreshing beverage, which has been used as a gargle for sore throats, may be made by crushing the berries and straining the juice. Indians also used its leaves and fruits as a poultice to soothe irritated skin.

Cashew Family (Anacardiaceae)

Quaking Aspen — *Populus tremuloides*

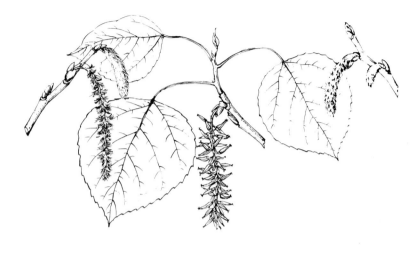

From C. S. Sargent, Manual of the Trees of North America

Native to the United States

HEIGHT: up to 60 feet or so (has reached 100 feet).

LEAVES: 1-3 inches long, slightly less wide, turning yellow in autumn.

This fast-growing, short-lived tree is very intolerant of competition and grows in open woods and clearings throughout the United States except in the Southeast. It is said to be the most widely distributed native tree in North America.

The Quaking Aspen is characterized by smooth, whitish or greenish-gray bark and leaves which tremble in the slightest breeze. The light, silky-haired seeds often are carried long distances by the wind, and they germinate one or two days after landing. This tree also reproduces by suckers which are abundantly produced along its long, shallow roots.

Willow Family (Salicaceae)

Lombardy Poplar — *Populus nigra* 'Italica'

Naturalized from Europe

HEIGHT: up to 90 feet, but usually much less.

LEAVES: somewhat triangular, 1-3
inches across.

The Lombardy Poplar, a narrow, columnar clone of the Black
Poplar, was introduced into the United States in the late eighteenth
century and since then has escaped from cultivation. It has been
widely planted as a fast-growing screen throughout this country,
but it is often troubled by borers and a canker which may cause
death before it is 10 or 15 years old.

Relatively large specimens of Lombardy Poplar are seen growing
wild on exposed sites in Boston, and young plants are found on many
vacant lots.

Willow Family (Salicaceae)

94

Gray Birch — *Betula populifolia*

Native to the northeastern United States

HEIGHT: up to 30 feet, usually with multiple trunks in a clump.

LEAVES: triangular, 2-3 inches long, turning yellow in autumn.

BARK: white, with triangular black markings.

Seedlings and small saplings of this native Birch are often encountered on vacant lots, but larger trees are less often found growing wild in Boston — perhaps because they are not able to compete successfully with fast growing grasses and herbaceous weeds. Gray Birch seeds are very light, and, like those of the Aspen and Poplar, may be carried long distances by the wind.

This fast-growing, short-lived tree is abundant on dry, gravelly, barren soil throughout New England. It springs up in large numbers on abandoned farmland and in areas that have been recently burned. Like other pioneer trees, it provides protection for seedlings of trees that will eventually constitute a forest.

This photograph was taken above Brigham Circle, where the Gray Birch grows in association with Pin Oak (*Quercus palustris*) in steep puddingstone cliffs.

Birch Family (Betulaceae)

95

Willows — *Salix* spp.

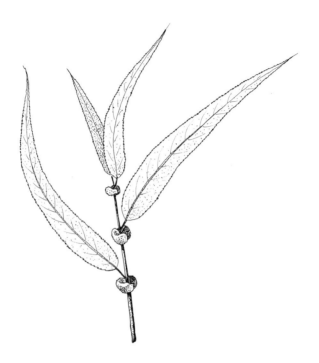

A variety of different Willows, grows wild in Boston. We have found at least five different ones, including both native and introduced species. As a group they tend to be associated with damp soil in low-lying areas, and they are generally rapid-growing, short-lived, and very intolerant of competition.

Willows produce large quantities of seeds which are carried long distances by the wind. This fact accounts for their presence on vacant lots far from seed producing trees.

While Willows have been cultivated widely, their inclusion in city plantings has been discouraged because their roots often clog drains and sewers.

Willow Family (Salicaceae)

96

97

Black Locust — *Robinia pseudoacacia*

Native to the Appalachians and some parts of the central United States

HEIGHT: to 70 or 80 feet, but usually less than 40 feet.

LEAVES: pinnately compound, of many oval, rounded leaflets 1-2 inches long.

FLOWERS: white, in Wisteria-like pendulous clusters in late spring, fragrant; followed by a cluster of narrow, Pealike pods.

    Besides its decorative value in gardens and parks, the Black Locust has had a practical significance in forestry as an excellent, temporary cover for old fields and land strip-mined for coal. It grows rapidly (4 feet or more a year on good sites) and is able to tolerate a wide variety of soils. In addition, it can pave the way for less tolerant trees by improving the soil it grows on. Soluble nitrates, calcium, magnesium and potassium are released in its litter of leaves and twigs which rapidly decompose, and nitrogen-fixing bacteria associated with its roots further increase the nitrogen content of the soil.

    Black Locust requires an open site to grow well, and will not tolerate competition from other plants. Its natural mode of reproduction is through the production of root suckers. Its seeds have very hard outer coats which are relatively impervious to water and do not germinate readily. However, some seedlings of the Black Locust do spring up here and there on open, sunny sites in Boston.

The Black Locust tree is distinguished by its deeply furrowed bark, thorny twigs, rich dark green leaves, and lovely, fragrant flowers. The wood is particularly resistant to weathering and thus was extensively used for fence posts. Despite its fine decorative characteristics, however, the Black Locust is no longer cultivated extensively in parks and gardens because of its susceptibility to injury from an insect known as the Locust Borer.

Legume Family (Leguminosae)

Honeylocust — *Gleditsia triacanthos*

Native to the Ohio and Mississippi Valleys

HEIGHT: to 70 or 80 feet.

LEAVES: lacy-textured; pinnately compound, of many leaflets ½-1 inch long.

FRUIT: long, narrow, flat, brown pods 1-1½ feet long.

In recent years, a thornless form of this tree that seldom bears fruit has become a popular tree for street plantings. The Honeylocust has an impressive list of characteristics that are considered important in urban conditions: it grows rapidly and is tolerant of alkaline soil, road salt, and drought; its lacy foliage casts light shade and does not obscure business signs; it creates minimal leaf litter to be raked up in the autumn.

In the wild this tree becomes established only in sunny openings, and, oddly enough, grows as a bottom land tree, preferring moist soil despite its reputation as a drought tolerant tree.

The seeds are scattered by animals, which feed on the sweet seed pods. The tough outer coverings of the seeds are softened (improving their chances of germination) as they pass through the digestive tracts of the animals.

While the native Honeylocust bear long, branched thorns sometimes reaching 4 inches in length, most of the trees planted in the city are thornless cultivars.

Legume Family (Leguminosae)

100

Ashes — *Fraxinus* spp.

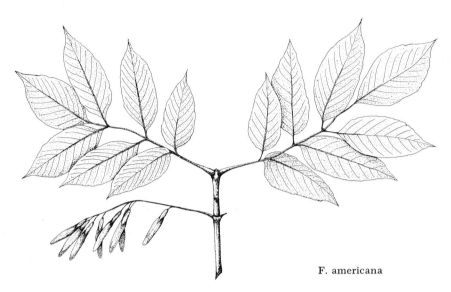

F. americana

Native to the United States

HEIGHT: 40-60 feet, but occasionally in excess of 100 feet.

LEAVES: pinnately compound, of 5-7 oval, pointed leaflets 3-6 inches long.

FRUITS: 1-2 inches long, slender, winged at one end.

Two native Ashes grow wild in Boston. The White Ash (*Fraxinus americana*) is a large, fast-growing tree, which appears as a pioneer on fertile, abandoned fields in some parts of Massachusetts. It prefers a well-drained soil and is somewhat exacting in its soil nitrogen requirements. Its seeds are not apt to travel far (up to 400 or 500 feet) but abundant seedlings are produced in the vicinity of mature trees.

The Green Ash (*Fraxinus pennsylvanica*) prefers damper locations than the White Ash, and is most commonly found on alluvial soils along rivers and streams. In Boston it is often encountered along unmowed sections of the Muddy River. Its seeds are dispersed by water and wind. This is the most widely distributed Ash in North America.

Both of these Ashes have been widely planted in the United States. The White Ash is a very large tree growing to more than 100 feet tall. It is identified by its erect form and distinctive but unusual autumn foliage, a unique blend of yellow, russet, and purple. The Green Ash is smaller and more rounded in shape.

Olive Family (Oleaceae)

102

Oaks — *Quercus* spp.

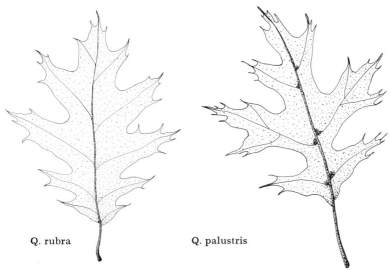

Q. rubra

Q. palustris

Young Oaks spring up near parent trees or at fair distances if squirrels have transported and buried acorns; if given half a chance these trees thrive in Boston. One of the best examples of active Oak regeneration in the city can be seen along the Muddy River, where the original Oak plantings have been allowed to go wild and now cover a rather extensive area.

By far the most common Oak to be encountered in Boston is the Red Oak (*Quercus rubra*), a handsome tree which is native to the eastern United States and has been widely planted in Boston parks and along its avenues.

The Pin Oak (*Quercus palustris*) is another native Oak which is common in the city. Unlike the Red Oak, it can tolerate wet sites, but it is more sensitive to competition from other trees. It is distinguished by its more deeply cut leaves (which turn scarlet in autumn), a distinctive pyramidal outline, at least when young, and drooping lower branches.

Beech Family (Fagaceae)

103

Maples — *Acer* spp.

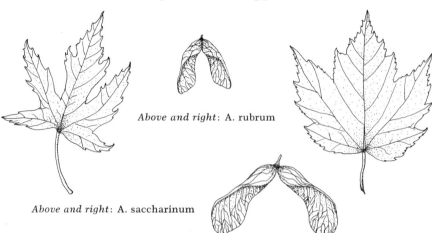

Above and right: A. rubrum

Above and right: A. saccharinum

Several different species of Maple spring up locally near parent trees here and there in Boston, but only two species are frequently encounterd throughout the city: the Norway Maple (*Acer platanoides*) and the Sycamore Maple (*Acer pseudoplatanus*). Both trees are aliens, brought to the United States from Europe in Colonial days.

The Sycamore Maple is the more rugged of the two. It almost rivals the Tree of Heaven in its vigor and adaptability, and is very often found in gardens and on urban lots. It is characterized by coarse, dark green foliage (resembling the Sycamore leaf in shape, hence its name), distinctive long clusters of winged seeds, and flaky bark.

The Norway Maple has been more widely cultivated than the Sycamore Maple in recent years. In fact, it has been one of the most widely planted street trees in the eastern United States during the past century. Its popularity has stemmed from its beautiful show of greenish-yellow flowers in early spring before its leaves are out, its yellow autumn foliage, and its fairly strong tolerance of difficult growing conditions. As its winged seeds ripen, they are showered over the ground below, and are found germinating in nearby gardens, gutters, or any shallow little pocket of moist soil the following spring. But the saplings of this tree are fussier about their growing conditions than those of the Sycamore Maple, and make their best growth in the moist fertile soil of open gardens.

Two other Maples are occasionally encountered locally in Boston. The Red Maple (*Acer rubrum*), a common tree in low woods throughout the eastern United States, is distinguished because of its brilliant red autumn foliage. The Silver Maple (*Acer saccharinum*) was widely planted along New England streets in the past, but its use has been discouraged because it attains a very large size and the wood is brittle. Seedlings of both these species are locally common in scattered locations, but mature trees growing wild are rare.

Maple Family (*Aceraceae*)

104

A. platanoides

Black or Rum Cherry — *Prunus serotina*

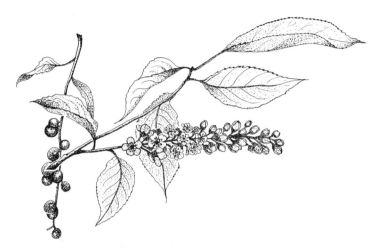

Native to the United States

HEIGHT: 15-40 feet, but occasionally to 90 feet.

LEAVES: lustrous, oval with pointed tips, 1½-6 inches long, with finely toothed margins.

FLOWERS: small, white, in slender, showy, drooping clusters 4-5 inches long; followed by small, black fruits ¼ inch or so in diameter.

This is a pioneering tree of secondary successions that cannot tolerate the competition for sunlight, moisture and nutrients in dense forests. It seems to grow best in slightly protected sites with moist, fertile soil, such as that provided by small clearings and the peripheries of thickets and woodland in the countryside. In the city it is most commonly found on the edges of gardens and parks, or in slightly overgrown areas.

The Black Cherry becomes particularly conspicuous in the late spring, when its long, narrow clusters of small white flowers come into bloom. These flowers are followed in late summer by clusters of small, black cherries which are edible and widely dispersed by feeding birds. Its fruits have been used to make jelly and wine, and also to flavor rum or brandy (hence its popular name, "Rum Cherry"). The wood has been prized for cabinetmaking since Colonial days, and as a consequence there are few large trees still to be found growing in the wild.

The Choke Cherry (*Prunus virginiana*), a similar species, also is found wild in Boston. Its fruits are acid and puckery, without the winey taste characteristic of those of the Black Cherry.

Rose Family (Rosaceae)

106

Buckthorns — *Rhamnus* spp.

Above: R. cathartica

R. frangula

Naturalized from Europe

HEIGHT: to 20 feeet.

LEAVES: roundish to oval, with toothed margins in the Alder Buckthorn, 1-3 inches long.

FRUITS: black, Cherry-like, borne singly or in clusters of 2-5.

The two Buckthorns that grow wild in Boston are the Common Buckthorn (*Rhamnus cathartica*) and the Alder Buckthorn (*Rhamnus frangula*), both introduced species. Several native species occur in the Northeast, but none has been seen in Boston.
The Buckthorns are large, coarse, rapid-growing shrubs with lustrous dark green leaves. They often appear in association with Black Cherry along the slightly overgrown edges of parks and gardens. They were originally introduced from Europe for use as hedges, and have escaped from cultivation to hedgerows, thickets and open woods throughout the eastern United States. Their seeds are widely scattered by birds, which are attracted to the shrubs by the berries. Since the fruits of the Alder Buckthorn ripen at slightly different times, there may be green, red and black ones all growing on the same plant at one time. The fruits of both species are violently purgative and should not be eaten.

Buckthorn Family (Rhamnaceae)

107

Elms — *Ulmus* spp.

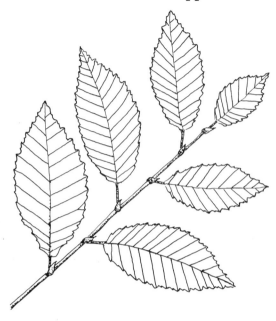

U. pumila

Elms are distinguished by their coarsely toothed leaves that are often lopsided at the base and rough on the upper surface. The Siberian Elm (*Ulmus pumila*) is the one most commonly found growing wild in Boston. This native of Siberia and northern China is a tough, rapid-growing tree eventually becoming as tall as 75 feet, that does well on dry, exposed sites with infertile soil. It has been widely planted in recent years, particularly in the Midwest, and has proved to be a valuable screen tree in drought-prone areas of the Great Plains.

The Siberian Elm, however, is rather undistinguished in appearance, and has neither attractive flowers, colorful autumn foliage, nor graceful shape to recommend it for general planting. In addition, the wood is brittle, and its abundant seedlings can be annoying. It might be distinguished from most other Elms by its small, 1 to 3-inch long leaves.

The American Elm (*Ulmus americana*), a native American tree, also is occasionally found as a volunteer in Boston. This very fine tree, with its graceful, fountain-shaped habit, is one of New England's most distinctive and widely planted shade trees. Unfortunately, it is highly susceptible to the Dutch Elm disease which is caused by a fungus.

Elm Family (*Ulmaceae*)

108

U. americana

Raspberries and Blackberries — *Rubus* spp.

Native to the United States

HEIGHT: to 5-6 feet, but usually much lower and spreading, often vine-like.

FLOWERS: to an inch or more across with 5 white petals, followed by sweet, juicy, dark reddish or purplish fruits.

Raspberries and Blackberries are widely distributed throughout the Northern Hemisphere. Many species are weeds of fields, roadsides, fencerows, and other open areas; others persist after cultivation around old homesites. All of them are prickly or thorny, and the more vinelike Blackberries, often called Brambles, are particularly unpleasant to walk through.

The "berries" of these plants are familiar and delicious. They are actually tight clusters of tiny fruits, each with a single seed. When Raspberries are picked, the central portion, a whitish, cone-shaped structure, remains on the plant. In Blackberries, this central portion does not separate from the fruit, causing the fruit to be somewhat tough in the center.

Rose Family (Rosaceae)

110

Ferns

Hay-scented Fern — *Dennstaedtia punctilobula*

Native to eastern United States

This is a common Fern in a variety of habitats, from shady woods to open, rocky pastures, in the eastern half of our country. It is rare in Boston, however.

Unlike the other plants treated in this handbook, Ferns do not produce flowers or seeds. They reproduce by spores which are borne in brownish spots of various shapes on the undersides of the leaves. In the Hay-scented Fern, the spore-spots are enclosed in minute cups located near the tips of the smallest lobes on the leaves.

The Hay-scented Fern is a somewhat invasive species, spreading by fast-growing underground stems. Its leaves, which are finely divided and up to 2 feet long, do not appear in clumps as do those of many other Ferns. Rather, they sprout individually along the underground stem. Their sweet scent, resembling that of fresh-mown hay or grass, is evident when they are crushed, and particularly so when dried.

Fern Family (Polypodiaceae)

112

Sensitive Fern — *Onoclea sensibilis*

Native to eastern United States

Ferns are uncommon in Boston, but this is the one most frequently encountered. It is a familiar plant in wet areas and low woods throughout New England. In Boston it is most abundant along the Muddy River, but the photograph above was taken on a series of cliffs on Mission Hill, quite an atypical habitat.

The leaves of the Sensitive Fern may grow to nearly a foot long. They are pale green in color and not as finely divided as in most Ferns. The spores are borne on separate leaves which are greatly modified in shape, without any obvious resemblance to the normal (sterile) ones. The whole structure resembles an upright cluster of small grapes.

This Fern is particularly sensitive to even the lightest frost, hence its common name.

Fern Family (Polypodiaceae)

Bibliography

Brockman, C. F. 1968. Trees of North America. Golden Press, New York.

DeWolf, G. P., Jr. 1974. Guide to Potentially Dangerous Plants. Arnoldia 34: 45–91.

Fernald, M. L. 1950. Gray's Manual of Botany, ed. 8. Van Nostrand Reinhold, New York.

——— & A. C. Kinsey. 1958. Edible Wild Plants of Eastern North America, rev. ed. Harper & Brothers, New York.

Georgia, A. E. 1930. A Manual of Weeds. Macmillan, New York.

Hatfield, A. W. 1971. How to Enjoy Your Weeds, American ed. Sterling Publishing, New York.

Hinds, H. R. & W. A. Hathaway. 1968. Wildflowers of Cape Cod. Chatham Press, Chatham, Mass.

Kingsbury, J. M. 1964. Poisonous Plants of the United States and Canada. Prentice-Hall, Englewood Cliffs, New Jersey.

Leighton, A. 1970. Early American Gardens. Houghton Mifflin, Boston.

Montgomery, F. H. 1964. Weeds of the Northern United States and Canada. Ryerson Press, Toronto.

Muenscher, W. C. 1939. Poisonous Plants of the United States. Macmillan, New York.

———. 1955. Weeds, ed. 2. Macmillan, New York.

Rickett, H. W. 1966. Wild Flowers of the United States; Vol. 1, The Northeastern States, McGraw-Hill, New York.

Salisbury, Sir. E. 1961. Weeds and Aliens. Collins Clear-type Press, London.

———. 1962. The Biology of Garden Weeds. Journ. Royal Hort. Soc. 87: 338–350.

Tobe, J. H. 1969. Proven Herbal Remedies. Provoker Press, Canada.

Wright, R. H. 1972. What Good is a Weed? Lothrop, Lee, and Shephard, New York.

Index to Plants Described

(Scientific names are in italics)

115

116

117